I didn't know that some snakes spit poison

© Aladdin Books Ltd 1997

Produced by
Aladdin Books Ltd
28 Percy Street
London W1P 0LD

This edition is published in 1999 by
Troubadour Limited
for the
Travelling Book Company
Ringwood, Hampshire

Concept, editorial and design by
David West Children's Books

Designer: Robert Perry
Illustrators: David Wood, Rob Shone and Jo Moore

ISBN 0-7613-0877-6

Printed in Belgium

I didn't know that some snakes spit poison

Claire Llewellyn

COPPER BEECH BOOKS
BROOKFIELD, CONNECTICUT

I didn't know that

snakes have scales 6

snakes lay eggs 8

some snakes move sideways 10

a snake smells with its tongue 13

snakes have fangs 14

some snakes spit poison 16

snakes have elastic jaws 19

pythons can live on one meal a year 20

some snakes have rattles 22

some snakes live in the sea 24

you can't charm snakes 26

some snakes can fly 28

glossary 30

index 32

Introduction

Did *you* know that snakes can hear through their jawbones?

... that most snakes are harmless?

... that the most poisonous snake in the world lives in the sea?

Discover for yourself amazing facts about snakes, from the tiniest that is thinner than string, to the mighty python that can polish off an entire leopard at one sitting...

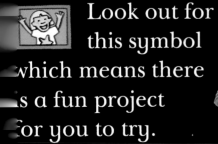 Look out for this symbol which means there is a fun project for you to try.

 Is it true or is it false? Watch for this symbol and try to answer the question before reading on for the answer.

I didn't know that

snakes have *scales*. Like all *reptiles*, snakes have dry, scaly skins made of a tough material like finger nails. The scales are watertight. They keep moisture in so the snake won't dry out in the heat.

Close-up of scales

Reticulated python

Try to find out the true facts about snakes. Touch one, and you'll discover that its skin is not slimy, but warm and dry. Also, far from being a danger, many snakes need our protection.

There are about 2,500 different kinds of snake.

Snakes have never been very popular. Many people are frightened of them. In the Bible story, it is a snake that tempts Eve to disobey God and eat the forbidden apple.

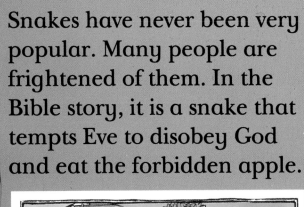

Agama lizard

Galapagos tortoise

 **True or false?**

Snakes are related to crocodiles.

Answer: **True**

They both belong to the reptile family. It's a large family with about 6,500 members. They're split into four main groups: turtles and tortoises; crocodiles and alligators; snakes; and lizards.

Nile crocodile

7

SEARCH & FIND SEARCH & FIND SEARCH & FIND

Can you find the lizard?

I didn't know that

snakes lay eggs. Most snakes lay soft, leathery eggs which they bury somewhere on land – in a hole in the sand or under a pile of rotting leaves. The eggs soon hatch into baby snakes.

Racer

Although most snakes lay eggs, some, such as vipers, are born live.

Baby snakes have a sharp tooth on their top jaw. They use this to cut their way out of their egg. Soon after they hatch the egg tooth drops off.

Egg tooth

King snake

True or false?
Snakes keep losing their skins.

Answer: **True**
As it grows, a snake's scaly skin becomes too small for its body. Every few months it sheds a paper-thin outer layer, which peels off like a long sock. Underneath, there's a shiny new skin in a larger size.

I didn't know that

some snakes move sideways.

Desert snakes move over the sand in their own special way. They make a coil in their body, and throw it across the ground. This is called sidewinding.

 True or false?
Snakes are *warm-blooded*.

Answer: **False**
Snakes are *cold-blooded*. They are not cold to touch but their bodies are only the same temperature as the air around them.

Sidewinder

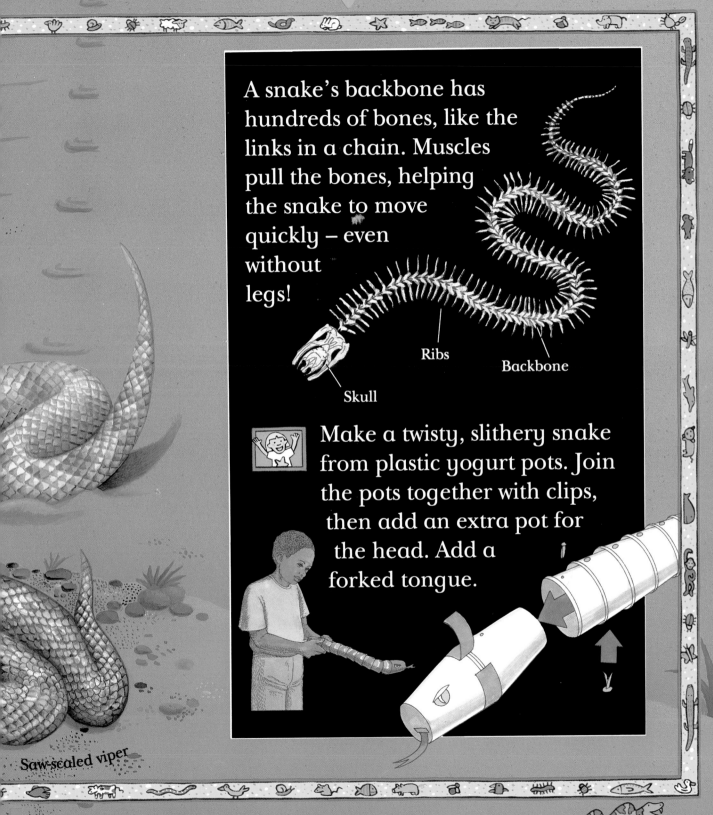

A snake's backbone has hundreds of bones, like the links in a chain. Muscles pull the bones, helping the snake to move quickly – even without legs!

Ribs

Backbone

Skull

Make a twisty, slithery snake from plastic yogurt pots. Join the pots together with clips, then add an extra pot for the head. Add a forked tongue.

Saw-scaled viper

The jumping viper can leap one metre up into the air.

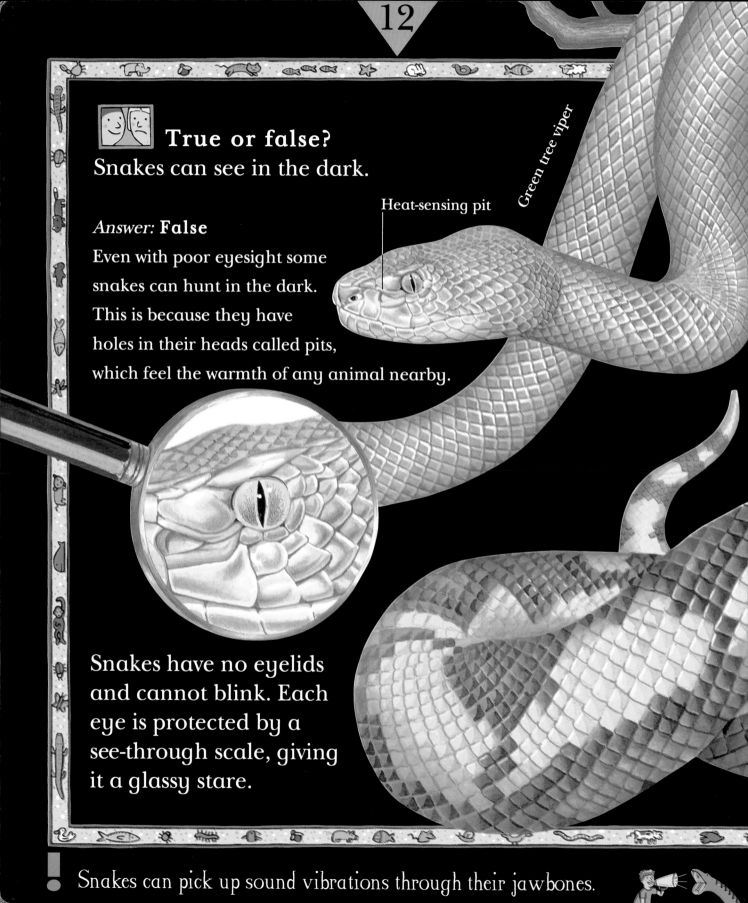

True or false?
Snakes can see in the dark.

Answer: **False**
Even with poor eyesight some
snakes can hunt in the dark.
This is because they have
holes in their heads called pits,
which feel the warmth of any animal nearby.

Heat-sensing pit

Green tree viper

Snakes have no eyelids
and cannot blink. Each
eye is protected by a
see-through scale, giving
it a glassy stare.

Snakes can pick up sound vibrations through their jawbones.

I didn't know that

a snake smells with its tongue. A snake's forked tongue picks up chemical messages from the air and the ground. These 'tell' the snake whether a meal, an enemy or a mate is near.

Jacobson's organ

A special part of the snake's body makes sense of all these chemical messages. It is called the Jacobson's organ and lies in the roof of the snake's mouth, within easy reach of its flickering tongue.

Carpet python

I didn't know that

snakes have *fangs*. Poisonous snakes have long, hollow teeth called fangs. When snakes strike their prey, they sink their fangs into the animal and inject it with deadly poison. When the snake eats its prey it is not affected by the poison.

Fang

Gaboon viper

Inside a poisonous snake's cheeks are *venom glands* – the animal's poison factory. As the snake attacks, its cheek muscles squeeze poison out of the glands, along a tube and out through the fangs.

Fang

Venom gland

Boomslang

Fangs

True or false?
Some snakes have fangs at the back of their mouth.

Answer: **True**
Back fangs take longer to poison prey than front fangs. The snake has to hold on and chew before the poison really starts to pump.

Fangs are rather like the hypodermic needles used by nurses.

I didn't know that

some snakes spit poison.

A threatened cobra will spray poison in its enemy's face. The poison causes burning or blindness if it hits the eyes.

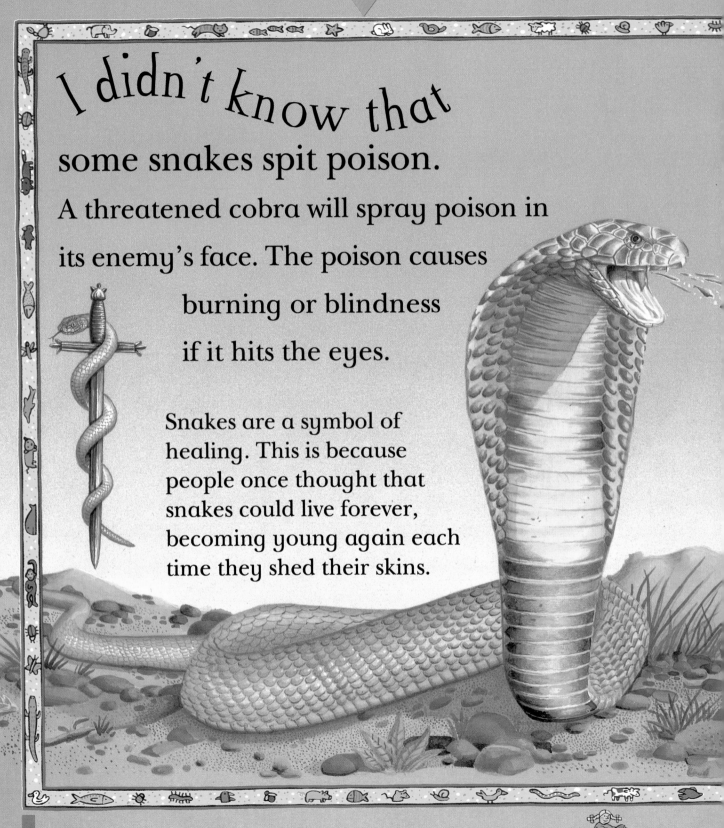

Snakes are a symbol of healing. This is because people once thought that snakes could live forever, becoming young again each time they shed their skins.

Snake venom is 'milked' to make medicine for snake bites.

The cobra was the symbol of royalty in Ancient Egypt.

Cleopatra was Queen of Egypt over 2,000 years ago. When Egypt was conquered by the Romans, she decided to kill herself. The story goes that she grasped a snake, called an asp, and died of its poisonous bite.

Mongoose

The British writer, Rudyard Kipling, wrote a story called *Rikki-tikki-tavi*, about a *mongoose* that saves a family from a cobra. Mongooses are fast and fierce, and are snakes' natural enemies.

Some fussy snakes will only eat other snakes!

This vine snake has caught a lizard.

 True or false?
There are no vegetarian snakes.

Answer: **True**
All snakes eat some kind of meat. Many of them have a varied diet, feeding on insects, worms, fish, frogs, lizards, birds and deer. People with pet snakes often feed them with live mice!

Some snakes have no teeth, so they swallow eggs whole. Such large mouthfuls could choke them, but the snakes push their *windpipe* forward and so keep their airway clear.

Windpipe

Snakes' jaws are joined at the sides by a bony hinge. This 'unhooks' during a meal, allowing the mouth to gape wide open. The bottom jaw is made in two parts which can separate.

Bony hinge

This stretchy material is called a *ligament*.

I didn't know that

snakes have elastic jaws. Snakes can swallow meals that are bigger than themselves. Their mouths open very wide because their skin is stretchy, and the bones in the jaws and skull can pull apart.

Egg-eating snake

It can take a snake as long as several hours to swallow a meal.

After a big meal, a snake has a huge lump in its body.

I didn't know that

pythons can live on one meal a year. Pythons kill their prey by squeezing it until it stops breathing. These huge snakes are strong enough to kill a leopard – and may not need to eat another meal for a whole year.

SEARCH & FIND SEARCH & FIND

Can you find the mouse?

20

True or false?

Snakes can hypnotise their prey.

Answer:

False

No snakes can hypnotise their prey. But in the film of Rudyard Kipling's *Jungle Book*, a giant python called Kaa tries to hypnotise animals with his swirling, colourful eyes. He hopes to put them in a trance and kill them – but he never actually succeeds!

Indian python

The mighty anaconda hunts *caiman* in the rivers of the South American rainforest. The snake lies in wait low in the water and then pounces on its prey – and hugs it in its coils until it dies.

! The emerald tree boa feeds on birds in tropical rainforests.

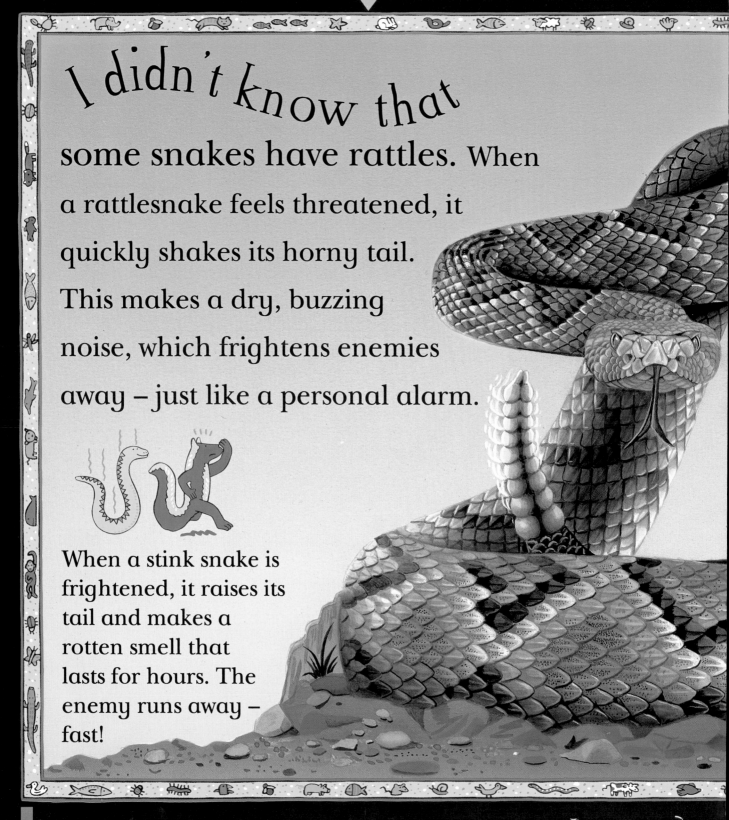

I didn't know that

some snakes have rattles. When a rattlesnake feels threatened, it quickly shakes its horny tail. This makes a dry, buzzing noise, which frightens enemies away – just like a personal alarm.

When a stink snake is frightened, it raises its tail and makes a rotten smell that lasts for hours. The enemy runs away – fast!

Most snakes avoid a fight. They prefer to slither away.

Coral snake

Milk snake

Some snakes fool their enemies by pretending to be more dangerous than they are. The milk snake is harmless, but it has the same skin colouring as the deadly coral snake – a disguise that must often save its life.

Rattlesnake

True or false?
Some snakes dodge danger by pretending to be dead.

Answer: **True**
When an enemy appears, the grass snake (below) lies on its back with its tongue sticking out. It looks very dead! A clever move because most meat-eaters prefer their meals fresh, and tend to leave dead animals alone.

I didn't know that

some snakes live in the sea.

There are about 50 kinds of sea snake. Some of them live near the shore, but others spend all their time out at sea, diving and coming up for air.

Horned viper

Can you find ten clown fish?

SEARCH & FIND
FIND & SEARCH

Many snakes live in the desert. The horned desert viper hides away from the midday sun by wriggling under the sand. It comes out to hunt at night.

Sea snakes have a flat tail, which they use as a paddle.

Snakes that live in cool places *hibernate* in winter.

Snakes in tropical forests hunt frogs, lizards and birds. Some forest snakes are green and hang from the branches like vines. Others have patterned skin, which hides them amongst the foliage on the forest floor.

Green mamba

Banded sea snake

True or false?

There are no snakes at all in Ireland.

Answer: **True**

People say that a Christian bishop, called Saint Patrick, believed all snakes were evil and banished them from the country. Saint Patrick lived over 1,600 years ago – but the snakes have never returned.

I didn't know that

you can't charm snakes.

Snake charmers seem to hypnotise their snakes with their pipe-playing. In fact, snakes are deaf and can't hear the music at all! To them, the pipe is an enemy, and they follow its sweeping movements to be ready to strike. Most of these snakes have had their poison taken out just to be safe!

SEARCH & FIND Can you find the stray snake? FIND SEARCH & FIND

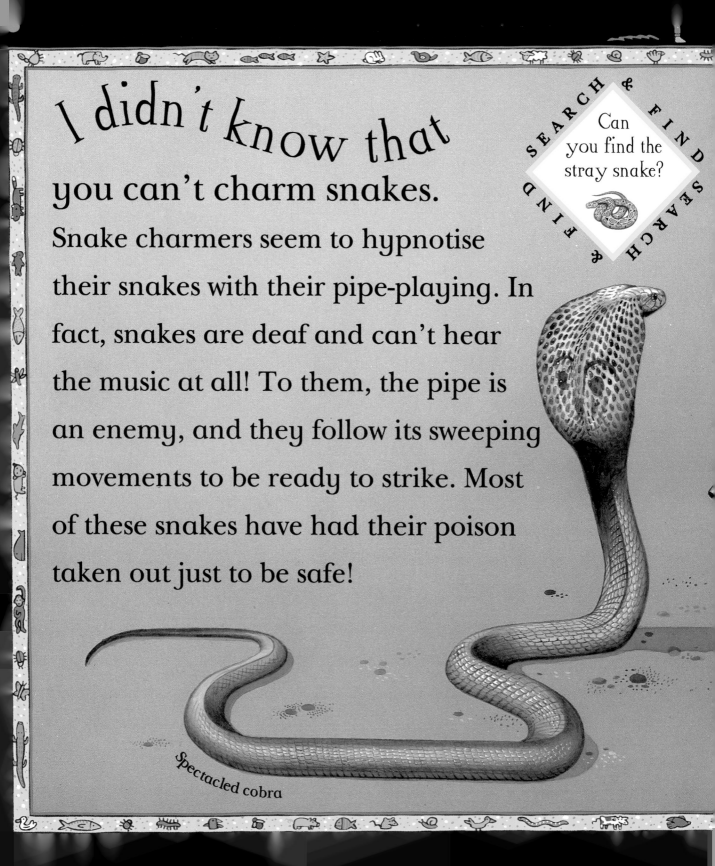

Spectacled cobra

True or false?
Snakes make good pets.

Answer: **True**
Many snakes are harmless and become quite tame if you handle them gently. Snakes are specially bred for pets, and are never collected from the wild. Their owners keep them in a container called a *terrarium*.

In the stories of Ancient Greece there was a monster called Medusa. She had snakes instead of hair, and anyone who looked at her was turned into stone.

Farmers like snakes because they catch rats and other pests.

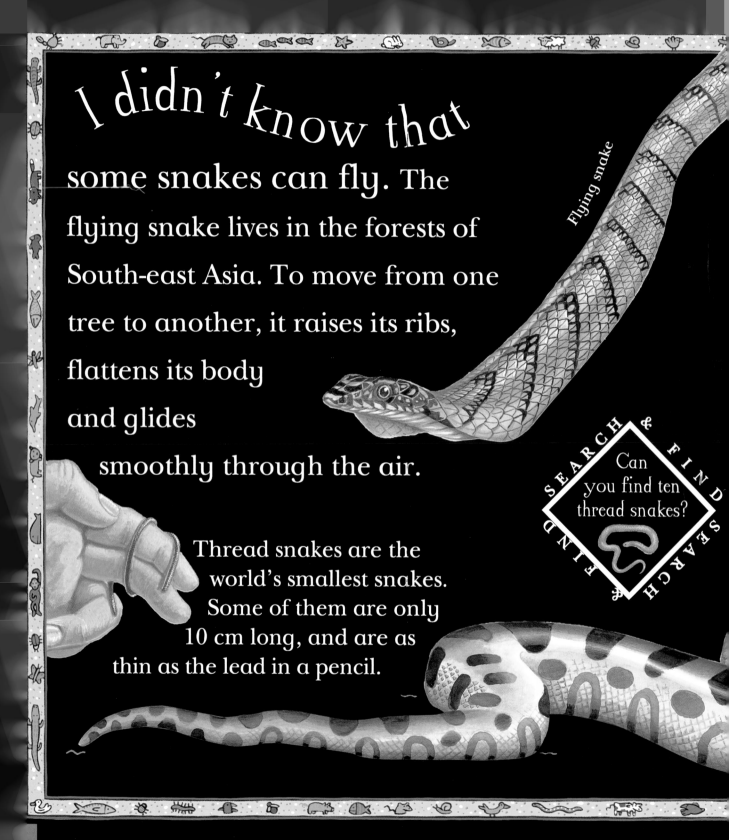

I didn't know that

some snakes can fly. The flying snake lives in the forests of South-east Asia. To move from one tree to another, it raises its ribs, flattens its body and glides smoothly through the air.

Flying snake

Thread snakes are the world's smallest snakes. Some of them are only 10 cm long, and are as thin as the lead in a pencil.

SEARCH & FIND
Can you find ten thread snakes?
FIND & SEARCH

Watch out for the African black mamba. It's the fastest land snake!

True or false?

Snakes live longer than people.

Answer: **False**

The oldest snake ever recorded was a boa constrictor called Popeye. Popeye lived in a zoo, where he was comfortable, safe and well-fed. He was 40 years old when he died.

Boa constrictor

The heaviest snake in the world is the anaconda. The biggest anacondas can weigh nearly 230 kg. This is as much as three men.

Glossary

Caiman
A type of alligator from Central and South America.

Cold-blooded
Cold-blooded animals have a body temperature that changes with the temperature outside.

Fang
A long, sharp, hollow tooth that poisonous snakes use to inject venom into their prey.

Gland
A part of the body that produces a special chemical substance, such as venom.

Hibernate
To spend the winter in a kind of deep sleep.

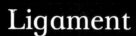

Ligament
A ligament is like a strap. It is made of tough material that holds bones in place at the joints.

Mongoose
A small, furry animal that is common in India. It is very good at killing snakes and rats.

Reptile

A member of a group of animals that includes snakes, lizards, crocodiles and turtles. Most reptiles have a dry, scaly skin and lay their eggs on the land.

Scales

The small, thin, plate-like pieces that cover the bodies of reptiles and fish.

Terrarium

A secure container in which people keep small land animals, such as snakes.

Venom

A poisonous liquid that snakes and some other animals inject in a bite or a sting.

Warm-blooded

Warm-blooded animals keep their body temperature at the same warm level, whether it is hot or cold outside.

Windpipe

The tube in the body which is an air passage between the throat and the lungs.

Index

anaconda 21, 29
asp 17

black mamba 28
boa constrictor 29
boomslang 15

caiman 21, 30
Cleopatra 17
cobra 17
cold-blooded 10, 30
coral snake 23
crocodiles 7

desert snakes 10

eggs 8, 9, 18
egg tooth 9
Egypt 17
emerald tree boa 21

fangs 14, 15, 30
flying snakes 28
forest snakes 25

forked tongue 11, 13

gaboon viper 14
grass snake 23

horned desert viper 24
hypnotise 21, 26

Ireland 25

Jacobson's organ 13
jawbones 12
jaws 19
Jungle Book 21

Kipling, Rudyard 17, 21

leopard 5, 20
lizards 7, 8, 18, 25

Medusa 27
milk snake 23
mongoose 17, 30

pet snakes 18, 27
pits 12
poison 16

Popeye 29
pythons 5, 9, 20, 21

rattlesnake 22
reticulated python 29
Rikki-tikki-tavi 17

Saint Patrick 25
scales 6, 31
sea snakes 5, 24
sidewinding 10
skin 6, 9, 16
snake bites 16, 26
snake charmers 26
spectacled cobra 26
stink snake 22

terrarium 27, 31
thread snakes 28
turtles 7

venom 15, 31
vipers 8, 11

warm-blooded 10, 31